A SOMERSHAM SCRAPBOOK

By
Alan Draper

All profits from the sale of this book will be donated to Charity

Published by Alan Draper

All rights reserved.

First Published 2020
© Alan Draper 2020

Printed and bound by

Somersham, Cambridgeshire

A catalogue record for this book
is available from The British Library
ISBN 978-0-9928565-4-0

Contents

INTRODUCTION

The making of scrapbooks has long been a method by which people have preserved memories for present and future generations. It can be a way to preserve old photographs and organize them and present them in a pleasurable, colourful and interesting way, as opposed to storing them in a box.

Over the last few years I have written and compiled a number of books relating to aspects of the history of Somersham and the life of people in the village. In the course of the research for these books I have been assisted by a number of local people several of whom have lent me photographs and other memorabilia. There is a good deal of material that I have not used so far and this book is an attempt to use it, particularly the photographs. However, the book is primarily based around the photographs and the text is peripheral, although I have included some written sections which I feel are interesting. The quality of some of the photographs is not very good as they are old, but I felt that they were still worth using for their historical value.

As I only came to live in Somersham in July 2006 all that I can write about is what have seen for myself, or what I have discovered through my research. I have learnt a great deal by talking to people who have lived in the village much longer than I have and in many cases for all of their lives.

The book is not comprehensive, in the sense that it is a rather a book of 'bits and pieces' and as such there many things which I have not been able to cover. I have tried to work under particular, and in some case familiar headings and there is no significance to the order in which topics appear. So, for example when covering shops I know that there were shops in other places, notably Church Street, that I have not mentioned purely because I have no photographs of them.

This book's theme is of how things in Somersham have changed. I hope that for many, the contents of the book will evoke memories of past times and for others, I will be helping them to discover things about the village, of which they were previously unaware.

ACKNOWLEDGEMENTS

I would like to thank my wife Jean for all the help and encouragement she has given me in compiling the material for this book. I am very grateful to her for proof reading the text and giving me advice on the content and format.

My thanks go out to a number of people who have allowed me to use their postcards and other photographs and also to those people in Somersham, who have provided me with much relevant information, either when I interviewed them, or just in casual conversation.

I am very grateful to the following people who have let me borrow photographs that they own: Graham Brooker, Malcolm Carrington, David Chambers, Howard Dolby, Len Dunster, Eddie Howlett, Ivy Kimber, Chris Leah, Stuart Marsden, Anne Pawson, Gill and Geoff Rowe and Dianna Skeggs. My sincere apologies to anyone who I have forgotten to include.

Finally I would like to thank Claire Callan who proof read my finished book very thoroughly and made many helpful suggestions which I have adopted.

AERIAL VIEWS

There are some interesting aerial photographs of Somersham that show us features of the village that have changed or even disappeared.

The view above shows Somersham in the wider landscape. One can easily see St Ives Road in the foreground and it is possible to pick out Church Street on the right and Parkhall Road on the left.

The photographs on the next two pages offer an interesting contrast between Somersham in 1950 and in 1990. The village had spread considerably in the intervening years with a great deal of new housing. Whitehall Close is on the left of the 1990 picture and the Grange Road estate is at the top and there were other new housing estates that are just off the photograph.

Somersham in 1950

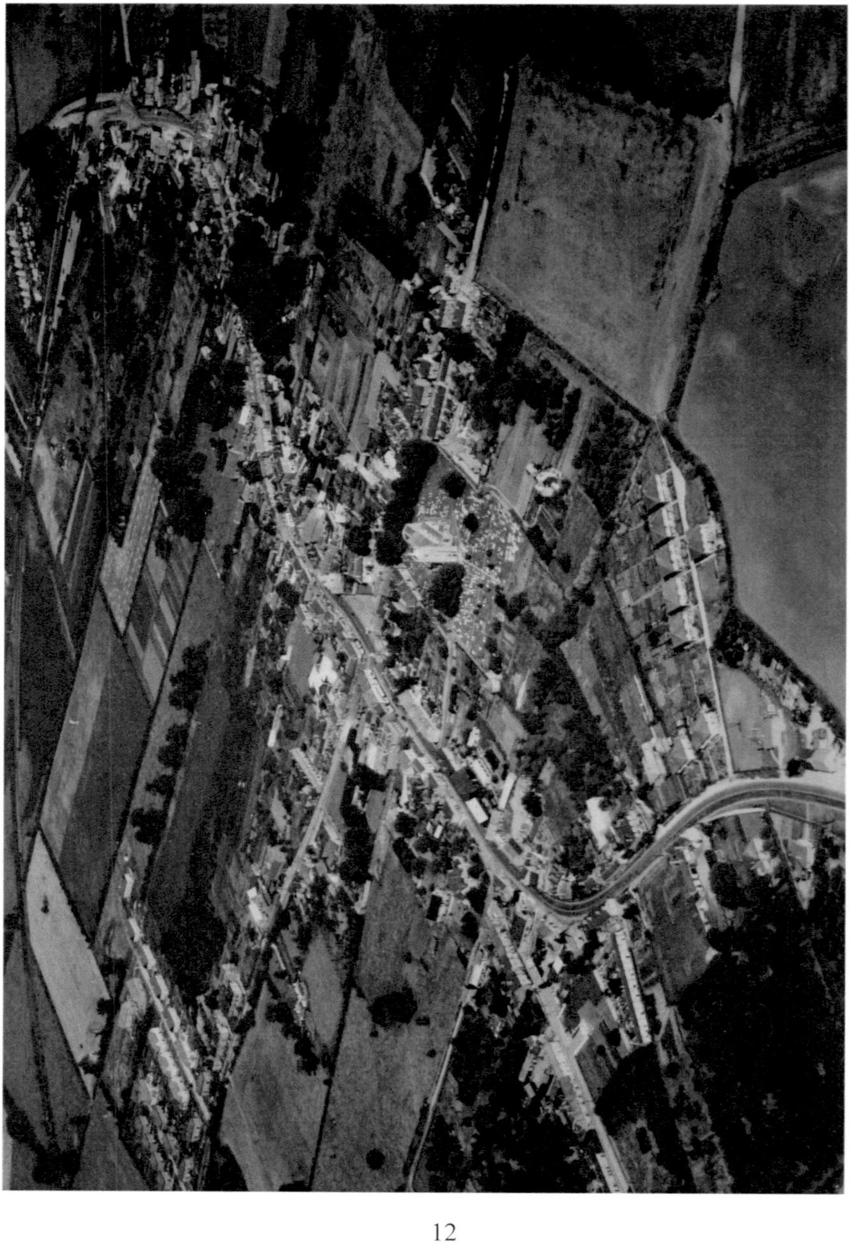

Somersham in 1990

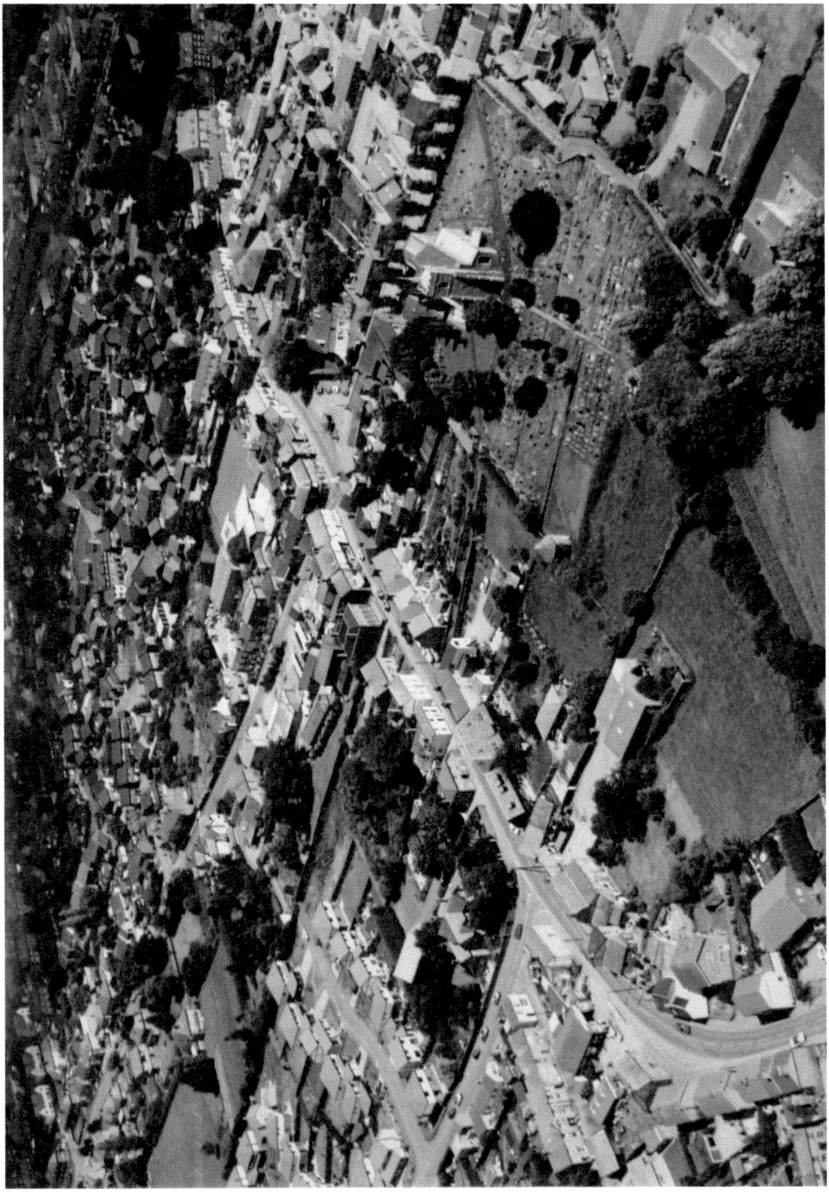

The photograph below centres on the junction of High Street, Station Approach, Colne Road and The Bank. The railway line, the station and the gas holder can all be picked out. There is no sign of Feoffees Road or the roads that branch off it today.

This view from the top of the Church Tower gives a more detailed picture of the centre of Somersham.

SHOPS

As the years go by there are fewer and fewer shops in Somersham. Even since I moved to the village in 2006 Bonnett's Baker shop and the butcher's shop have closed to be replaced by an estate agents and a florist's shop. We have seen a mini supermarket open (Tesco Express), but that was at the expense of the Black Bull public house. Additionally another pub, the George, has been converted into living accommodation.

We must be thankful that we still have a chemist, which sells all manner of goods, a post office in a grocery store and the afore mentioned mini-supermarket.

In my first book (Somersham Heritage) I wrote about some of the shops that had served the village in the past.

This old photograph (which probably dates from the 1950s) shows some of the longest serving shops in the High Street; Bonnetts Bakers, a general store, and on the corner opposite the Rose & Crown, the main part of Norman's Department Store.

The shops changed their appearance and ownership over the years. The general store was originally run by Walter Webb, and

15

later Bernard Haynes, although I knew it as a One Stop shop and now it is a Costcutter shop.

The One Stop Shop in 2008. It was a subsidiary of Tesco and it ceased trading not long after they opened their mini supermarket in the former Black Bull pub.

CHARLES NORMAN & SON

(E. C. Norman)
UNIVERSAL STOCKISTS
SOMERSHAM, Huntingdon
Telephone : Somersham 215

Your Local General Store at your service !

Main Departments :

* **Drapery**	* **Provisions** * **Hardware**	* **Furniture**
* **Boots and Shoes**	* **Floor Coverings**	* **Gents' Outfitting**

Charles Norman & Son was a department store which traded from different properties, the main shop being on the corner of Parkhall Road and the High Street. Since it closed in 1972 the shop has traded in various guises, most recently as a flower shop and it is now a coffee shop.

Left: The original shop.

Below: The shop as a Greengrocer's and Household store in the 1980s.

On the next page: As a florist's in the 2010s.

Norman's furniture shop was on the other side of the Cross, a site which later became a bank and is now a hairdressing salon.

Until March 2007 there was a shoe shop which was run by Ingrid Chambers from the annex of Hereford House.

HEREFORD
INGRID CHAMBERS
HOUSE
67 High Street, Somersham Cambs.
SHOES
Telephone: Ramsey 840233

The Sweet shop in the High Street was very popular, but it closed in 1988. May Elmore, who ran the shop, used to give packets of cigarettes to servicemen returning to their units.

J. LINFORD & SON
HIGH CLASS BUTCHERS
SOMERSHAM

Fresh Meat delivered daily to your door
Poultry all the year round
Smedley's and Findus Frozen Foods
Home fed Pork a Speciality
Pork Pies to order

Judging by the number of adverts that I have come across in old publications, there were a good number of butchers in the village in the past. Unfortunately we lost the last one in February 2018. One former butcher's shop was J. Linford & Son in the High Street, which later became an 'open all hours' convenience store, but has now ceased to trade as a shop.

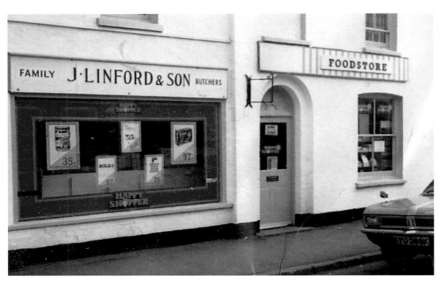

Some names of butchers that may mean something to very elderly Somersham residents are W.H.Gotobed, F.Parsons, Saint Bros. and Skeggs & Son.

W. H. GOTOBED, Jun.
FAMILY BUTCHER,
HIGH STREET, SOMERSHAM.
Families waited upon and supplied at shortest notice.
Tongues, Oxtail, Salt Beef and High-class Sausages always ready.

A. SKEGGS & SON,
Family Butchers,
Church St, Somersham.
Primest Beef, Mutton, and Home-fed Pork.
Lamb and Veal in Season.
Noted Shop for SAUSAGES and LARD.

A butcher, trading more recently, was Trevor Buddle whose shop was in Feoffees Road (now Penny's Beauty Salon). Note that Trevor supplied meat for deep freezers.

TREVOR G. BUDDLE
FAMILY BUTCHER AND
DEEP FREEZE MEAT SUPPLIERS
FRESH AND COOKED MEAT ON DISPLAY AT
EOFFEES ROAD SOMERSHAM TELE. RAMSEY 84207
ALSO AT STATFOLD GREEN WARBOYS
TELE. RAMSEY 822344

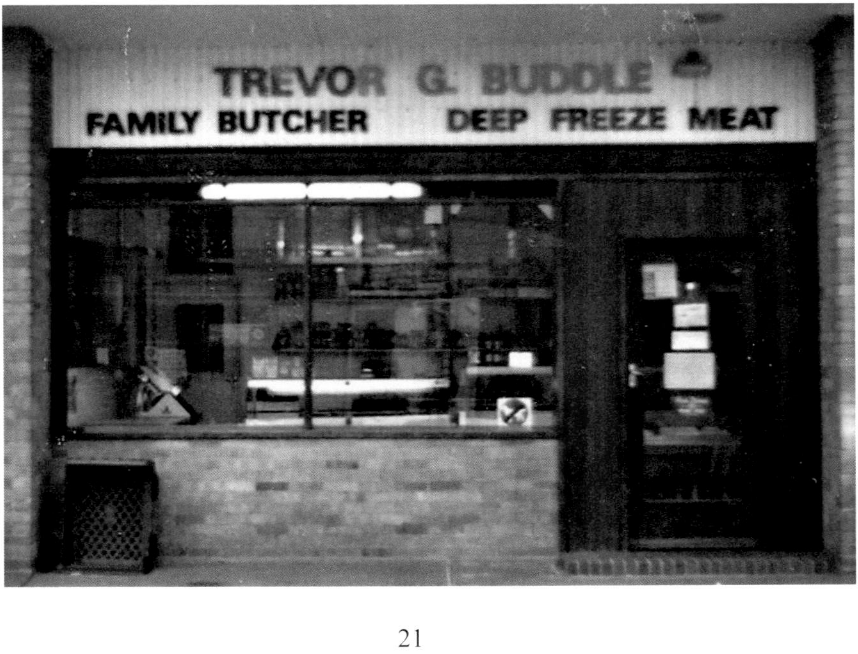
TREVOR G. BUDDLE
FAMILY BUTCHER
DEEP FREEZE MEAT

The frontage of Pauline Haylett's shop was probably typical of many of the shops that used to be in the High Street.

One of the oldest photographs of a Somersham shop that I have been given belonged to Harry Lane. It is possible to make out a penny-farthing bicycle on the right hand side of the picture.

The invoice on the right is dated 1898 and although the items are written in pencil it is possible to make out the following:

Sugar 7½d
Lard 5d
Wax 2½d

Unfortunately it is not possible to see the quantities of these products and the other ones on the invoice.

It is believed that the photograph below shows the original shop before it expanded.

Whilst on the topic of shops there was a commercial office, that of Charringtons Coal Merchants. It was adjacent to number 31 High Street and was still in use by Charringtons in the early 1980s after which it was used for horology. However it is believed that it was originally used as an office for the registration of births, marriages and deaths.

The shop/office of Twinseal Windows Ltd run by Gordon Southon is shown here near the Cross on the north side of the High Street, the building occupied today by Impressions the printers. Later Gordon moved over the road to the premises that is now a barber shop.

FINANCIAL PREMISES

Today we have the Post Office and an ATM (automated teller machine) or 'hole in the wall'. Once there were at least two banks and a building society office in Somersham. Barclays Bank was in the High Street next to Linford's shop; Lloyds Bank was on the Cross (now a hairdressing salon) and there was an Estate Agents in Church Street that offered insurance and building society services

The TSB also operated their bank on two days a week from the rooms on the left hand end of Wisteria House, the house in the High Street with a monkey puzzle tree.

Brumar Insurance Services was at 91 High Street next to the Black Bull public house which is now Tesco Express. It was run by Bruce Baker and his wife Mary. Later Mary ran a tearoom from these premises, it is now a private dwelling.

SOME OTHER SOMERSHAM BUSINESSES

This building belonging to William Canham (Building Contractors) does not seem to exist in Somersham anymore although I believe that they operated from somewhere in the High Street and built a considerable number of the council houses in this and other villages, including all the houses in Bank Avenue.

T. W. Lumley Ltd was a building firm that built several small housing developments in Somersham including Hammond Way, King Street and The Pastures.

Another business that operated in Somersham for a long time was Huckles, which did egg packing and was situated in Parkhall

Road near the Fish and Chip shop. The photograph below shows some of the men who worked for Mr Huckle in front of their fleet of vans.

There are a number of companies that operate on the West Newlands Industrial Estate on St Ives Road. Why Newlands? On the 1887 O.S. Map there is a large area labelled Newlands. My guess is that this land was once marshy and when it was drained it became new land. There is still a drainage ditch that runs that side of St Ives Road.

John Nind (Pest Control) originally leased the land from the District Council and initially had a block of six units built on it. Later they were occupied by a number of people, including Stuart Marsden and Peter Tyers. All of the occupants grouped together and brought the freehold on the land. Peter also built a seventh unit on the end of the block.

Stuart Marsden ran Somersham Pottery from November 1978 until October 2003. A major part of the production was circular customised wall plaques to be mounted on the exterior wall of a property. During the time that the pottery was operating, over 10,000 plaques were produced and beside the local market they went all over the UK and were exported to ninety different countries. Stuart also made the chimney pots for the restoration of Somersham Park House which were made to match the last remaining damaged pot on the house.

Two examples of the popular wall plaques made at the Pottery that can be seen on many buildings in the area.

Len Dunster bought a unit from one of the other owners, he had a small independent car repair shop for servicing and mechanical repairs, which he ran from 1995 until 2012. That unit has now been let to Tom Dolby from where he runs Tom's Cakes.

Some of the original units on the industrial estate.

Inset: Len Dunster with a Humber Super Snipe.

Peter Tyers still has his unit which is a workshop where he carries out welding, fabrication and ornamental ironwork.

Above: Peter Tyers and his son Jason looking under the bonnet of an old Daimler Consort.

More, larger buildings have been built on the estate since the original units were set up. Companies come and go covering a range of different manufacturing and services. There have been double-glazing window and door companies, engineering works producing air rifles and a commercial printer. A long time occupant is Imotek International Ltd who offer sales and service support for a wide range of veterinary ultrasound scanners for all small and large animal applications.

SOMERSHAM'S OLDEST DWELLING HOUSE

Cranbrook Farm undoubtedly holds that accolade. The house is timber framed with a thatched roof and brick gable end and has a 19th century two storey gault brick house-like addition at one end. It was originally built about 1492 and it has undergone a

considerable process of restoration since it was first bought by its owners Malcolm and Margaret Carrington. The photograph on the left shows what it was like when they first saw it and the picture below shows it when the roof had been removed.

The first stage of the restoration was to more or less take the building apart and turn the old beams into a massive jigsaw puzzle and build it up again. They started the rebuild in 1992. This involved taking the building apart carefully and systematically, numbering the timbers in order to facilitate reconstruction. Many new timbers had to be cut and shaped to replace those which were no longer usable and they were all put together with wooden pegs, not nails.

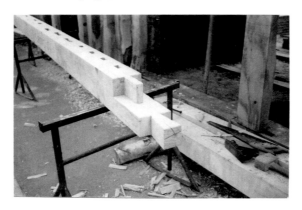

When they bought it the house had conventional windows, but bearing in mind the age of the property this was not historically correct. The house would have had mullions, simple holes, originally with shutters rather than glass. This would have allowed the smoke from a fire in the middle of the floor to escape. The chimney would have been a later addition.

This photograph shows the skilled carpentry in all its glory. The walls then had to be constructed with wattle and daub, which is a woven lattice of wooden strips called wattle and this is daubed with a sticky material usually made of some combination of wet soil, clay, sand and straw.

The restoration took ten years to complete. It was a mammoth undertaking and not without considerable problems at times, but a wonderful achievement.

Above: The newly thatched framework, as seen from the rear of the house.

Below: The front of Cranbrook Farm today.

THE PARISH CHURCH

The oldest building in Somersham is the Parish Church and over hundreds of years the people of Somersham have maintained and developed it, as is still the case today.

Most of the building as we know it today was built between 1250 and 1300.

In the 14th Century the roof was raised to make a clerestory and a timber roof supported on stone corbels was constructed. A series of bosses were also carved on the intersections of the purlins and could depict the life of Adam Easton a former Rector of the Church although this has not been confirmed. The North Porch was also built at the end of the 14th Century.

One of the stone corbels   *One of the carved roof bosses*

In the 15th Century the South Porch was added with wooden outer doors, a Stoup for Holy Water was built into the corner of the North Porch and leaded windows were added to the South and North aisles and to the East window in the Chancel.

In the 17th Century a sundial on a pedestal was added to the gable of the South Porch and a weather vane was sited on the Tower.

In 1782 a set of 6 bells cast by Edward Arnold of St Neots were mounted on a wooden frame which is believed to be older and probably for the original bells.

In the 19th Century the stone font, given by Rev. Alfred Ollivant, D.D., Regius Professor of Divinity at Cambridge and Rector from 1842 to 1849, was positioned in the centre aisle at the west end of the Nave.

In 1864 the Tower Clock was installed.

In 1885 an extension was built to house the organ that had previously been sited at the west end of the Church.

In 1895 the chimes were added to the clock.

In 1902 the bells were re-hung and repairs were made to the tower.

In 1908 a new pipe organ was installed by Cousans, Sons & Company of Lincoln which is still in use today.

In 1912 central heating radiators were installed and benches from the Chancel were converted into pews.

In 1915 a new parquet floor was laid and a stained glass window to the west side of the north aisle was dedicated.

In 1922 the stained glass in the three slender lancets at the east end were designed by Thomas F. Curtis as a memorial to Somersham men who lost their lives in the 1914-18 war.

In 1927 the Church was reordered and the furniture replaced with modern pews, pulpit and choir stalls a gift from Mrs Stanley Nix and family.

In 1931 Chancel Roof timbers were replaced.

In 1936 a new heating boiler was installed.

In 1949 a scheme was approved to install electric lighting to replace the gas lighting. An electric organ blower was installed, although the original hand bellows were retained.

In 1961 a new gas boiler was installed.

In 1970 the church was closed in June for urgent repairs to the roof after deathwatch beetle was found - it re-opened in December.

In 1979 more work was needed on the Nave Roof.

In 2005 the removal of rust and repainting of down pipes and gutters was undertaken. There was replacement of tiles on the south side of the Chancel Roof, pointing and masonry repairs to the south clerestory wall, re-glazing of the south clerestory windows using the old glass but using new lead in the windows. The organ loft floor was replaced, the organ dismantled and cleaned, the great sound board, which suffered water damage, was rebuilt. The south aisle roof lead which was originally laid in 1878 was replaced.

In 2008 the pews at the west end of the Church were removed to make the church more versatile in its usage.

In 2013 major improvements were made to the west end of the Church, including an oak and glass screen enclosing the base of the tower to include toilet facilities and a meeting room. A purpose built refreshment area was added. Solid oak doors were installed at the entrance to the South Porch and oak, glazed internal doors were installed between the Nave and both the South and the North Porch.

In 2016 a new lighting scheme in the interior of the church was installed by placing lighting units in the nave spandrels and on tracks in the aisles and chancel.

Quinquennial repairs to the fabric of the building were also carried out. These consisted mainly of re-pointing, lead flashing repairs and replacement of some sections of stonework. Solid oak doors were installed at the entrance to the North Porch.

In 2017 the Chancel Roof was completely re-tiled with Welsh slate.

In 2018 the heating system was replaced with a new gas fired heating system, including the introduction of two boilers mounted on the wall of the North Porch, the introduction of low finned radiators, eight fan convectors and four column radiators.

In 2019 an access platform in the bell room was installed for safer access to the tower roof. Work to the Tower Clock including repainting and re-gilding the clock dial, cleaning the dial works and chime unit, work to the hammer squares and hammers, the introduction of guides to the winding units and a new motor were all carried out.

This labelled drawing of the church was done by Jack Rolph in 1993.

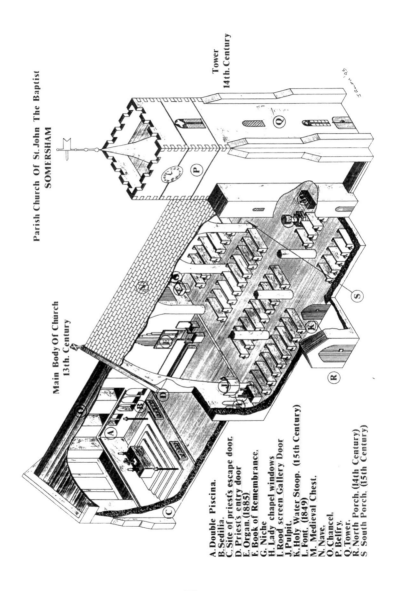

Parish Church Of St.John The Baptist
SOMERSHAM

Tower
14th. Century

Main Body Of Church
13th. Century

A. Double Piscina.
B. Sedilia.
C. Site of priest's escape door.
D. Priest's entry door
E. Organ. (1885)
F. Book of Remembrance.
G. Niche
H. Lady chapel windows
I. Rood screen Gallery Door
J. Pulpit.
K. Holy Water Stoop. (15th Century)
L. Font. (1849)
M. Medieval Chest.
N. Nave.
O. Chancel.
P. Belfry.
Q. Tower.
R. North Porch. (14th Century)
S South Porch. (15th Century)

THE CHURCH CLOCK

The clock has an interesting history. It was installed in 1864 by Willson & Woodruff who were watch and clock makers in Somersham, although it is believed that the clock would have been made in London. The history of Willson & Woodruff can be traced through the entries in trade directories, census records and the inscriptions on their two adjacent headstones in the churchyard not far from the tower.

Thomas Willson is first listed in a trade directory in 1839, when he was 29 years old. By 1864 he had a partner in Thomas Woodruff who at some time became his son-in-law, marrying Thomas Willson's daughter, Jane. Thomas Woodruff took over the firm some time between 1885 and 1890 and Thomas Willson died in 1891, aged 81. Thomas Woodruff died in 1914, aged 71.

It is fairly certain that their watchmakers shop is now the China Garden Restaurant in Somersham, as census records show it between Braunston House at the Cross and a baker's shop (more recently a butcher's shop). There was also a Woodruff's Yard next to the shop which today is the alley between the China Garden Restaurant and the old butcher's shop. There were two dwellings in this yard but in the 1911 Census one was called Garden Cottage, High Street, while the other was uninhabited.

The clock's Westminster Chimes were added in 1895. They were a gift from a Dr. Nicholls as a memorial to his wife, Edie Rowley Nicholls. They were put in by Messrs. Thwaites & Reid of Clerkenwell, London at a cost of £80 and were dedicated and started on 10th December of that year.

In 1935 the clock was stopped on 16th June through the

impertinence of a bird, which chose the works of the clock as its sanctum for hatching a family.

The following entries from the Church Parish Magazines all relate to the clock.

In May 1938 it was recorded that James Darrington *(who was blind)* had wound the church clock for a quarter of a century.

In March 1974 "The PCC is most grateful to the Somersham Feoffees and the Parish Council who have made contributions to cover the cost of the complete mechanical overhaul of the Church Clock". Permission to carry out the work was announced in the August Magazine and in the November Magazine the work was said to have been completed.

In April 1978 – An appeal for £7,000 to carry out essential repairs to the Church was launched. It included the re-gilding of the clock dial.

In 1988 the PCC decided to electrify the clock winding mechanism at a cost of £1,625 which was paid for by the Somersham Feoffees.

Recent overhaul

In 2019, the Parochial Church Council decided to get the clock mechanism completely overhauled and the dial on the tower cleaned, repainted and the hands and numbers re-gilded. According to church records no formal maintenance had been carried out on the clock for as long as anyone could remember, probably as long ago as 1974. This date had been recorded on the clock frame. The clock was no longer keeping good time and needed frequent adjustment. The cost of all of the work was over £10,000 and with the help of grants from a number of organisations and some of the Church's own funds the job was done in September 2019.

Above: The photograph above shows the main part of the clock mechanism.

Below: The dial is removed prior to renovation.

43

Removing the dial of the clock

CHURCH ROOF REPAIRS

The photographs below show the work on the roof of the Nave when it was re-tiled in 1970.

This was before the Health & Safety at Work Act came into force. Compare these pictures with the work on the Chancel Roof when it was re-slated in 2018.

Re-slating of the Chancel Roof in 2018

Below: The roofer is fixing slates to the wooden battens, the stone parapet is just behind him.

VILLAGE PUBLICATIONS

Regular news and information about events in Somersham probably started with the publication of the Church Parish Magazine.

The first Parish Magazine was produced for January 1875, it cost 1d. It began: "Dear Friends, We wish to bring before your notice a cheap, interesting and instructive magazine. It is published monthly; and we propose to make it of local interest by devoting space to publish matters ...."

In December 1876 there was an announcement that the number of magazines sold was so small and it was not receiving the general support that it did at first and it would be discontinued.

The Parish Magazine appears to have been re-launched in January 1891 as the 'Somersham, Pidley-cum-Fenton & Colne Parish Magazine', because the churches in the three villages constituted a benefice under the charge of the vicar.

The magazines not only contained information about church services, baptisms, marriages and burials but general news about the things going on and other items of interest.

Copies of the magazines are all stored in the church, many of the early ones bound together as proper books.

I have read through all of the magazines and on the following pages are some of my favourite extracts.

15th December 1892 was the burial of Ann Dring who had she lived another month would have been 104 years old. She had 3 children (all living) 29 grandchildren, 60 great grandchildren and several great, great grandchildren. Her eldest son was 76 and the youngest 60.

November 1895 – The Vicar regrets that the magazine is very far from being a success financially. He calculates upon a deficiency of about £6 at the end of the year, and fears it may have to be given up then. Do the parishioners wish this to be done, or will they assist the Vicar to bear the burden?

January 1897 – On the Festival of St Thomas, coals were given away to 12 persons in connection with the charity known as 'Johnston's'. The trustees only had 11s. 4d. at their disposal and each family received 1 cwt. On the same festival 68 lbs of meat were distributed among 26 widows and 8 widowers in connection with Wilson's Charity, each receiving 2 lbs. The trustees having in hand £1 16s 8d. have gone a little beyond the sum at their disposal, or at least were unable to increase the number of recipients.

February 1899 – Mr Whiteman, Somersham Stationmaster for 17 years has 'removed' to Whittlesey. He was presented with an address on vellum bearing 98 signatures and a purse containing 16 sovereigns at a dinner at the Rose & Crown.

March 1901 – A report on the death of Queen Victoria and the accession of King Edward VII.

October 1906 – The School Buildings have been greatly improved in having new stoves and fireplaces and the classrooms painted and coloured. 'As arrangements are being made to convey the children residing in the outlying Fen on Chatteris Road to school, we hope to see greatly improved attendance.'

April 1907 – A BATH CHAIR has been purchased for the use of the sick and infirm of the whole Parish. The following rules must be kept for its loan.

1. Application should be made at the Vicarage.
2. A grown-up (or responsible) person must fetch it and bring it back. Not children.
The Chair must be returned clean, and within the time agreed upon when it is borrowed.

N.B. – It cannot be lent out on wet days.

August 1912 – Somersham School - Headmaster and boys congratulated on again winning the Silver Shield for best kept school garden in the county.

August 1913 - The Vicar and Churchwardens again venture to remind parishioners that they cannot permit hand carts wheelbarrows etc to be pushed through the churchyard. The parishioners "right of way" through the churchyard gives the right to walk through but does not extend to any vehicles. We therefore appeal to the parishioners to support us in our endeavour to keep the Churchyard in decent order.

November 1916 – Mrs Tennent passed away on 29th September 'so recently married'. 'She was not well when the marriage took place, but we understand that her health showed some improvement for a few days. But a breakdown soon intervened, which proved fatal. As Miss L. Ibbott she was known from childhood in Somersham.' 'We offer our respectful sympathy to her sister and life-long companion, and also to her husband who gained and lost a wife within so short a space of time.'

August 1922 – A report of a Sunday School Outing to Hunstanton.

October 1936 – The Rector reports that "our new boiler responded very well to its first "Test". Heated by a relatively small fire, every radiator was hot in under three hours and no "bangs".

April 1937 – The Rector writes "I feel very impressed by the possibility opened up to us by the application of scientific discovery to take an actual part in the solemnities connected with our Sovereign's Coronation. The occasion is surely unique. By means of a wireless set or installation every Church and every home may become an annexe of the Abbey of Westminster on the Coronation Day with opportunities of hearing perhaps even more clearly than the worshippers in the Abbey itself".

October 1939 – The Rector writes "After the long suspense of the past months we find ourselves once again plunged into War, and no one can tell what the end of it will be. We know that it was not of our seeking, and that the greatest efforts were made to avoid it, but all in vain."

May 1941 – The Rector writes "The Parish Council have authorised the formation of a fire watching organisation for Somersham, and the Feoffees are providing some apparatus for use in the village. I have undertaken to organise the new body, and should be glad to hear from any lads of sixteen and over who are willing to take their share in this work. They will receive instruction in the best methods to deal with fires, and will provide much greater security for all in the village."

November 1942 – The Rector wrote about the worst disaster that has befallen Somersham for many years, when the plane crash on 5th October destroyed six houses and resulted in eleven deaths besides several cases of injury.

January 1949 – The PCC approved a scheme for the installation of electric light in Somersham Church and an electric blower for the organ.

May 1950 – The PCC decided to have the interior of the church cleaned and re-decorated which will cost nearly £100, and the report of the Organ Builder is that £140 must be spent on the organ to make it quite satisfactory but there were no accumulated funds to meet the costs.

June/July 1953 – The Rector writes about seeing the Coronation on television.

June 1959 – The top of the spire, with its weather vane, has now been dismantled for close investigation and parts of it have been brought down into the church. Apparently the spire was built in 1763 and then repaired in 1863. We can reasonably expect our present repairs to last another century.

January 1967 – Cost of the Parish Magazine increased from 4d to 6d as it had been running at a loss for years and this together with increased costs of printing left no option but to raise the price.

November 1970 – The Rector wrote 'the repair and renovation of the Church Roof is near completion. Our Parish Church has been closed since the beginning of June, we are looking forward to the re-opening of Somersham Church.

October 1972 – The Rector suggested that something like £250 a year, or £5 a week, should be set aside for church repair, maintenance and improvements. 'A glance at the collections shows that we come nowhere near this target.'

June 1979 – Congratulations to the organisers of the Carnival Weekend for providing for the village a full and comprehensive programme of activities to suit all tastes.

July 1980 – A report on the Flower Festival says that Sunday afternoon saw the first performance of the re-formed Somersham Town Band. "It is pleasing to see that after a gap of 20 years the people of Somersham are still willing to support their own town band."

There are no more magazines after 1982 in the Church. I believe that further publications were produced on an office duplicator and were not kept.

SOMERSHAM VOICES
At the end of 1999 Somersham Parish Council issued the first edition of a quarterly community newsletter called **Somersham Voices**. It was delivered free to every household in the village. Each issue started with a Parish Council Report and then there

were contributions from local organisations as well as from individuals including letters and emails to the editor and items of historical interest. It had a format that consisted of articles in boxes that were bordered with different types of design. Somersham Voices ran for 50 issues, the last one appearing in March 2012.

![Issue 37 - Dec 2008 of Somersham Voices newsletter]

SOMERSHAM4U

In 2012 the Parish Council then decided to move to a bi-monthly newsletter and it launched **Somersham4U A Voice for the Community** with the April/May edition. It had a more commercial feel to it, printed on better quality paper, with good quality photographs and title banner for each page. In 2018 the newsletter started to have a full page cover photograph.

THE PALACE

Whilst studying an old map of Somersham I noticed a building in the High Street labelled 'Picture Theatre'. Older residents have told me that it was called 'The Palace'. Today we know it as the Royal British Legion Hall.

This old photograph of the building with its sign over the doorway 'The Palace Social Club' is the best I have come across.

The building was formerly an old London Chapel which Bernard (Berni) Criswell purchased before the Second World War and had moved to Somersham. It was used for weekly cinema shows and for darts and dances. During the war the Palace was requisitioned by the army and after the war Berni sold it to his brother Joe, who later sold it to the British Legion.

This is a programme for the cinema shows

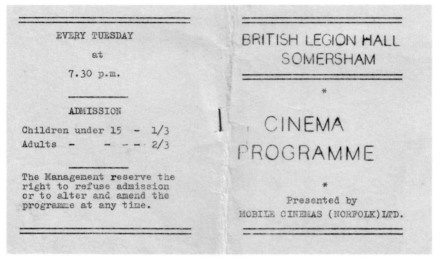

and the type of films that were being shown.

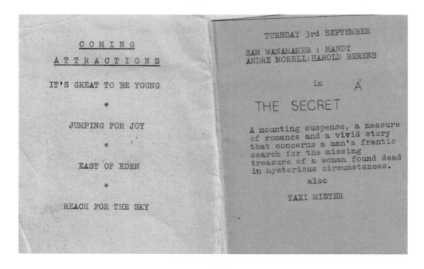

54

THE BALLAST HOLE

When the railway line was constructed in the middle of the 19th Century the company carrying out the work discovered a seam of gravel which provided enough ballast for the track from Somersham to Ramsey. Hence the Lake was known for many years as the Ballast Hole or by its abbreviated name the 'Bally-hole'. When the gravel was removed, the hole filled with water and it became a lake suitable for swimming and for skating when frozen in the winter.

Note the railway trucks, the water tower and the signal box in the background of the photograph of the swimmers.

It would seem that cattle and horses could be found around the Ballast Hole.

I have even seen a man practising his ice hockey skills on the lake when it was frozen.

The windsurfer gliding across the ice in this photograph was probably much more unexpected.

SOMERSHAM RAILWAY STATION

The railway and the station were of great importance to the village for over 100 years. The original station was erected about 1848, but many alterations took place afterwards.

The railway through Somersham closed in 1967 and some of the buildings were demolished and some parts were vandalised.

In 1977 the station buildings were bought by Sir William McAlpine who had them dismantled and taken to his estate at Fawley, near Henley-on-Thames where they were reconstructed.

Below: Somersham Station re-built at Fawley.

The station was very nicely kept with flower beds and floral displays. Here is a photograph of the railway staff (circa 1953/54).

What a shame that only one of these photographs is in colour!

There must have been a great air of excitement on the platform when youngsters were waiting for the train to take them off for a day at the seaside - probably Hunstanton.

THE WINDMILL AND THE WHITE POST

Although there were originally three windmills in Somersham, the most significant one was probably the one known as Holdich's Mill. It stood not far from the junction of Pidley Road and St Ives Road not that far from the White Post.

It had been operated by several generations of the Holdich family, John Holdich being the last. In this photograph of the mill John can be seen seated on the cap of the mill.

This very old photograph with the mill in the background shows the relative position of the mill to the White Post.

Holdich's Mill passed into the ownership of Mr. A. Kimpton and was eventually pulled down in 1922 thereby closing a chapter in the village.

Most people in Somersham will be familiar with the sight of the White Post, but not everyone will have taken that much notice of the oak tree behind it.

However, there is a piece of history relating to the tree. Inside the front cover of the Church Baptism Register 1889 – 1916 there is the following inscription:

An oak tree was planted near the White Post Somersham on Pidley Road – the gift of the Vicar Rev. W.S. Beevor on March 13th 1903 to commemorate the Coronation of King Edward VII on 9th August 1902. Mrs & Misses Beevor & several Parishioners were present.

The White Post is what is known as a guide post and it is a scheduled ancient monument. It is clearly marked with the date of the year of the Turnpike Act - 1773. Two hands on it point to 'Huntingdon through Pidley' and 'St Ives' respectively. There is no distance in miles on the post.

Such guide posts have been known for many years as in a 'A Direction for the English Traveller' published in 1635. The author remarks *"It is a usual manner, in many parts where ways be doubtful, for a traveller to find a standing post with a hand to direct men the ready way .... These hands tell thee not how many miles, nor the distance from place to place"*.

Above: The Windmill Public House gets its name because of its proximity to the site of the mill.

GARAGES

These days we tend to buy fuel for our cars at supermarkets or at one of the petrol stations run by the major oil companies such as BP and Shell. Cole and Day's garage, the only one serving petrol in Somersham is one of the relatively few independent petrol retailers in existence today. I wrote about some of the garages in the village in 'Somersham Heritage' but have subsequently found out more.

In 2014 I interviewed Dick Clements when he was almost 100 years old. He ran a garage with Ralph Brooker for many years after WW2. Dick Clements worked for Walter Brudenell for two years before the war.

Phone 203.

WALTER BRUDENELL,

Everything for the Car, Cycle and Radio.

Electric Lamps and Fittings.

District Agent for Raleigh and Humber Cycles.

CARS FOR HIRE.

SOMERSHAM, Huntingdon.

Walter's garage was I believe on the site of Cole & Day's garage. Dick and Ralph Brooker worked for him for a year after the war, before they set up on their own. Dick said that Walter Brudenell did a lot of work servicing agricultural machinery during the war and collected all sorts of agricultural odds and ends, because of its value. The garage was full of things that Walter had collected. It was everywhere, even in the roof. You could barely get a motor in. Dick took out all the rubbish and cleared out a couple of bays to get two motors in and over the weekend Walter put it all back. Dick thought "You're not going to change", so he decided to start up on his own. Walter stopped working soon after Dick and Ralph left. Stan Simmons took over the garage and Bert Barnes ran it for him.

Left: Here In this photograph Harold Saint is holding a horse while it is being shod by Ralph Brooker Snr.

Ralph Brooker's father, also named Ralph, had a Blacksmith's business in the High Street where Feoffees Road is now. It had a shed at the side with a forge in it. Ralph Brooker Senior was killed on a motorbike in the war.

I am not certain whether Dick and Ralph Jnr. set up their garage where the Blacksmiths had been or not. If they had, they would have had to leave in the mid-1950s when buildings were pulled down in the High Street to create the opening for Feoffees Road. Dick and Ralph rented a site at the west end of the High Street for a while, later it was rented by Hunts T.B.A. (Central Tyre Company).

This photograph was taken when the site at the west end of the High Street was being cleared.

Brooker and Clements moved on to build a garage at the High Street end of Feoffees Road, close to where the blacksmiths had been and ran a garage there until 1984 when it was sold to the owner of Bridge End Garage. Today the houses there are called Brooker's Place.

Left: A photograph of Brooker & Clements Garage with Ralph Brooker and his Vauxhall Velox.

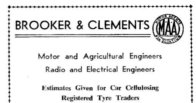

Returning to the subject of blacksmiths, Somersham once had up to five blacksmiths when horses provided the main source of power. In between the two World Wars there were only two such businesses and of course now there aren't any. In addition to Ralph Brooker Snr., John Henry Rilett and his son John had a workshop next to the Baptist Chapel in the High Street. Their workshop closed in the late 1940's. *See photograph below.*

One further garage that deserves a mention is West End Garage.

Although it no longer dispenses petrol, it was fascinating to see the old style petrol pumps with signs such as Shell, Esso and Cleveland before the West End Classics show room was built.

This old photograph shows the garage with Dew's classic Coach on the forecourt.

CHATTERIS FERRY TOLL

The boundary between Chatteris and the Parish of Somersham had been marked by a river known as Old West Water. When this was diverted, the old river bed became the road and it was on this road that there was a turnpike (toll gate) for about 200 years.

THE FERRY TOLL, CHATTERIS

Turnpike Acts authorised a trust to levy tolls on those using the road and to use that income to repair and improve the road.

The old postcard above shows the toll gate, the toll cottage and on the other side of the road the toll board showing the charges. Unfortunately the writing on the only photograph of the toll board is almost illegible.

Chatteris Ferry Toll closed on 24th June 1949.

The photograph above shows that another building was erected on the Chatteris side of the boundary. It operated as a public house 'The Blue Ball' for many years, later becoming known as the 'Crafty Fox'. Below is a very old photograph of when it was the Blue Ball.

PARK HOUSE

Park House is a Georgian country house with a Victorian annex which was built on the site of the Bishop's Palace in 1802. It is situated at the far end of Church Street.

During the Second World War the house was used by the army.

After the war the house fell into disrepair and became derelict. The photograph above shows how it looked early in the new millennium. The front façade lead had split enabling the guttering to leak into the brick work and internal timbers. A nine brick height difference had emerged due to subsidence from the north to south gable. Ivy had taken a hold on the south west gable, spreading through to the north east of the building. All the floors were in the cellar and little of the internal features remained.

A Demolition Order that had been placed on the house was lifted in 1984 after the intervention of the Georgian Society and in 2002 Richard & Janine Johnson purchased the house and work on the building commenced. Over a period of two years a complete restoration of the house took place. On Christmas Eve 2003 they moved into the house and it became their family home.

Above: The state of the rear of the property before restoration.
Below: The rear of the property after restoration.

The Georgian fascia of the building is now exactly as it would have looked when first built in 1802.

Below: The staircase before and after restoration.

THE LOCK UP AND FIRE ENGINE STORE

The old postcard picture below of Church Street shows a small brick building in the road just outside the Church gate. It was known as the 'lock-up', although it was actually a building which originally housed the fire engine. At the far end, however, there was a section where people could be imprisoned for a brief period before being taken to Huntingdon. The 'lock-up' was later used for storage and eventually removed in 1950.

Below: Somersham Fireman with their fire engine outside the Church

The fire engine was not really an engine at all; it was a 'Merryweather' pump on wheels and operated by four men each side to power the pump by reciprocal action. The team used to have a test run which the children watched with great pleasure. On one occasion there were so many holes in the hose, caused by rot or rats, that very little water reached the nozzle. At that time it was an honour to be included in the team, as your name was painted on the door for all to read. The old 'Merryweather' stayed in service until replaced by a 'Coventry Climax' pump in 1940.

Apparently when there was a flood under the railway bridge the firemen used to go down there for a practice with the engine and pump it out.

BRITISH LEGION PARADE

On Sunday 18th May 1969 members of Somersham British Legion paraded their new colours after a dedication ceremony in the church. After many years of service their old standard was handed over for safe keeping and a new standard dedicated.

The ceremony at the Parish Church was conducted by the Rector (The Rev. T. W. Jones) who received the old standard in the presence of a large congregation.

Making a parade worthy of the occasion, the branch was supported by representatives of both sections of the branches in the county. Twenty-eight standards made a colourful and impressive sight as the parade marched behind the Band of RAF Wyton.

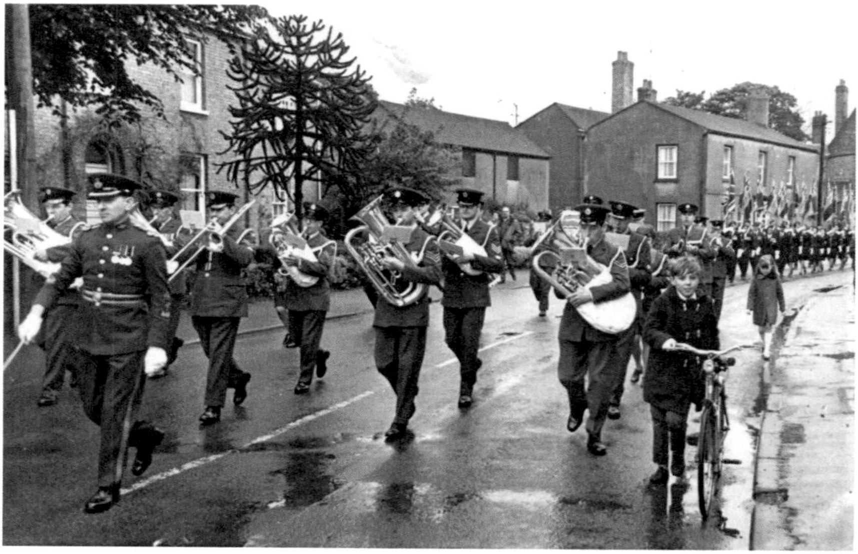

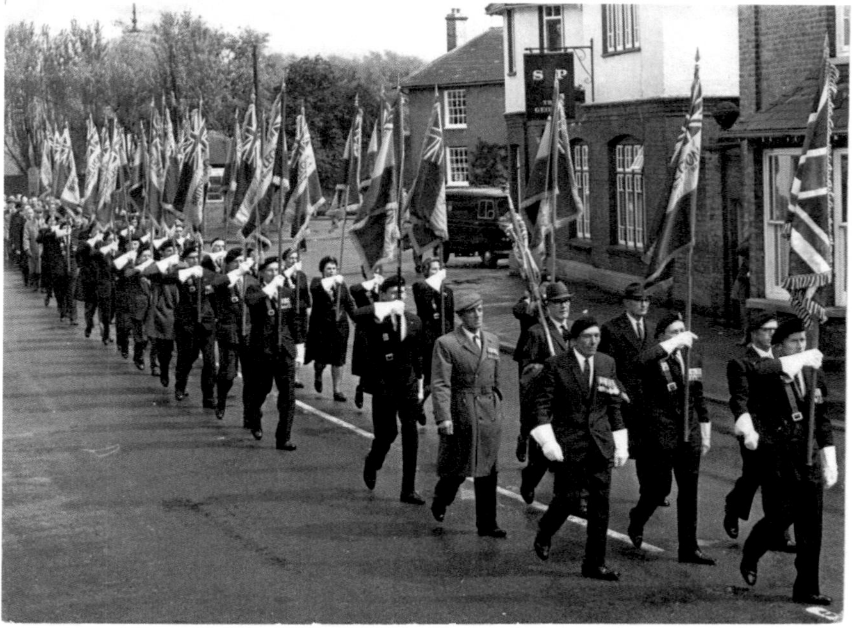
S P

SCHOOL PHOTOGRAPGHS

School photographs have been taken for a very long time as these early examples show.

The first two photographs are of classes in a school in which the teachers were Mrs. Betsey Frampton and Miss Clara Frampton.

Kelly's Directory for 1898 records that Mrs. Betsey Frampton was running a private school for girls. Amazingly she was about 78 years of age and her daughter Clara was 35 years old. It can be assumed that the old lady in the centre is Mrs. Frampton and the lady at the back is Miss Frampton. However, clearly there are boys as well as girls in the photograph, so is it possible that Kelly's Directory got it wrong? Betsey died in 1917, aged 97 and is buried in the churchyard in an unmarked grave.

Successive copies of Kelly's Directory show that Betsy continued to run the school until at least 1914, but the 1920 directory shows that the school was run by Miss Clara Frampton and in 1924 was taking boys and girls. The school's last entry was in 1931.

The photograph over the page shows Miss Frampton when she was running the school by herself.

Below: The girl in the centre of the front row is holding a board with 'Somersham Church School' written on it. It could be that this is the school in the building next to the Church and perhaps the Master is Nathan Dews who wrote 'A History of Somersham'.

These pictures show classes probably in the 1950s.

School photographs have now spread to those of school staff.

This shows the staff of Somersham Primary School in 1989.

THE BOYS' & GIRLS' LIFE BRIGADE

The photographs below show the second annual inspection and display of the 1st Somersham Company of the Boys' Life Brigade which took place on May 28th 1926. The Company had been formed two years beforehand.

This photograph of the Girls Brigade in Somersham probably
dates back to the 1940s. It was run from Somersham Baptist
Church. It is assumed that the gentleman in the middle is the
Baptist Minister and the ladies either side of him ran the
Brigade, one of them being his wife.

SOMERSHAM TOWN BAND

The village of Somersham has boasted a band since 1850 but the Somersham Town Band was not formed until 1918 just after the First World War.   Below are very early photographs of   the band.

In 1940 it was temporarily disbanded. The Band was entering contests as early as the 1950s, but unfortunately by 1962 the increasing competition of television had led to it being disbanded again.

This is a post war photograph of the Band.

In 1980 David Chambers, the current Musical Director, persuaded by some young players from the local primary school, reformed the Band which has gone from strength to strength ever since.

Above: The first practice when the band was reformed in 1980.

The Town Band has had various uniforms over the years. When it was reformed they had red jumpers, then came red jackets with black lapels with a gold trim. The current uniform has black jackets with red lapels with a gold trim.

Centre: The Band were Champions of Cambridgeshire in 1993.

In 1992 the Band toured Germany playing at a number of venues.

The year 2020 is the 40th Anniversary of the reforming of Somersham Town Band.

THE CHURCH CHOIR

At one time church choirs were quite large in number with boys, and later girls, as well as adults. The first of these photographs is believed to show the Church Choir in 1913.

Below is a much more recent photograph taken around 1980.

Above: The Church Choir in about 2000

Church choirs tend to be much smaller these days often with no children. At the present time the choir in Somersham Church numbers less than ten adults and there are no youngsters.

Choral singing is still popular, but they tend to be community choirs. In our area the Meridian Singers, which although based in Bluntisham, has a good number of Somersham residents as members.

SOMERSHAM CARNIVAL

The Carnival started in 1977, the year of the Queen's Silver Jubilee. Over the years, volunteers have run this popular event and sought to provide something that is fun and a source of revenue for local organisations. Initially the activities took place over one weekend but this later extended to a 'Carnival Week' beginning on a Saturday in June. Various events take place during the week and it all culminates on the following Saturday with the Carnival Parade going round the village and then there are stalls and events on the Norwood Field and in the Victory Hall.

Above: Floats assemble in The Trundle for the parade around the village streets, the lead float carrying the Carnival Princess and her attendants.

In addition to the floats there are people walking along with donation buckets, a parade of vintage cars, which are later judged and given awards and often it includes a marching band.

This early carnival photograph shows Somersham Town Band playing as they stride out along Feoffees Road in 1982.

Below: Vintage cars drive through the High Street

Floats in the High Street.

The youth organisations in Somersham like the Cubs and Brownies and the Playgroups decorate the floats and local businesses provide the trucks and other vehicles.

Above: Stalls ready on the Norwood Field - Carnival 2013

Below: General Scene - Carnival Day 2013

THE VICTORY HALL

Fundraising for a village hall to mark the Allies' victory started just after the Second World War. However, for a number of reasons building the hall did not start until the winter of 1986/87 and it was completed in 1991.

Above: The area is cleared ready for construction

Below: The steel framework is almost complete

Above: The framework complete.

Below: The start of bricking up.

Above: The building almost complete and the driveway and car park being prepared.

Below: The Victory Hall as it is now.

The Victory Hall was officially opened on 17th December 1991

by the Rt. Hon. John Major who was the local MP and Prime Minister at that time.

Below: John & Norma Major and Mick Hoy (Chairman of the Victory Hall Committee) and other guests

The hall is a popular facility and is more or less fully booked by local clubs and societies during the week and for private functions at the weekends.

TWO SPECIAL PEOPLE

I want to draw this book to a conclusion by writing about two important people whom I am glad to say that I have had the privilege to meet and who have had a significant impact on Somersham and further afield.

Harriett 'Hattie' Skeggs was a fairly formidable character. She was born in 1921 and lived her entire life in Somersham and served the local community as a District and a Parish Councillor as well as being actively involved in many aspects of village life.

I met her twice, once at the inaugural meeting of the Somersham History Society when she reminisced about life in the village, but I only got a chance to speak to her briefly. As I was carrying

out research for a Heritage Exhibition I wanted to speak to Hattie further so I wrote to her to ask if I could visit her to talk about village history.

It was a most interesting and amusing meeting. Although she was not very well physically, she was as bright as a button mentally.

She told me a bit about the things she had done, like in the war when she worked at a laundry in Hemingford. It was a reserved occupation because they cleaned Army and Air Force uniforms. Every day she cycled to Hemingford and back for work. After the war Hattie looked after her mother until she died. They were living at the Hammer and Anvil Public House in the High Street with her brother Leonard. She managed the pub until it closed as licensed premises around 1953. Later Hattie had applied for a post in the Cambridge City Housing Department and was selected for the position of Housing

Officer. She remained there until her retirement.

Hattie told me that she loved the Parish Church where she was a chorister and a bell-ringer; she also wound the clock and raised the flag on the tower. She told me about one hazardous incident when she had let go of the rope that was used to hoist the flag and it swung away from her, so she climbed on the tower parapet and clung on to the flag pole whilst reaching out to grab the rope.

Hattie was an active member of the Conservative party and was a Parish Councillor from 1964 to 2003 and a District Councillor from 1987 to 1995. She was obviously well versed in the history of the village and she told me that when she had been door to door canvassing in Crane Close for an election, she had been shocked that at some houses they had signs with cranes (the bird variety) on them. When I said that Crane Close had been named after John Crane, the first schoolmaster at the school, she retorted "You know too much". It seemed to amuse her that I knew some fairly obscure Somersham history.

I am told that Hattie was extremely involved in the life of Somersham, working tirelessly for the benefit and good of all. She did a great many things for local people on an individual level, as well as a councillor.

One thing that amused me was the fact that she used to send her dog with a basket along the road to Bonnett's Bakers Shop and it would return with a loaf of bread in the basket.

Hattie suffered her first stroke in 2004, after that she suffered a number of others and many small TIAs. After her last serious stroke in August 2010 she was hospitalised for six weeks and sadly when she came back home she could no longer walk. Being bedridden was very frustrating for such an active person and was a sad way for her to die.

In August 2012 David Bonnett unveiled the historic map of Somersham branded affectionately by the Parish Council working group as 'Hattie's map'. The map which stands in

Church Street incorporates the village as it is today together with the old names and places plus photographs. Hattie had been helping a working party from the Parish Council to put the map together using her in-depth knowledge of Somersham and its historic names. Sadly she died in July 2011, before it was completed.

 The Reverend John Galbraith Graham MBE was a British crossword compiler, best known as 'Araucaria' of The Guardian. John lived in Somersham for twenty years or more and he was a hugely respected man, not only because of his fame as one of the best writers of crosswords in this country, but also because he took an active part in the life of the Church and of the village. I only knew John towards the end of his very eventful life, mainly because he sang in the Church Choir and he occasionally preached and took services. However, as the years passed I got to know more about him and had some delightful conversations with him.

John always stood in the pulpit in the Church when he preached, which most preachers don't do these days, and although he was quietly spoken, I can't remember him ever using a microphone. You hung on every word because his message was so intelligent and interesting.

In spite of his fame John was a humble man, one of the most lovely you could wish to meet. Even when his second wife Margaret died of a heart attack in 1993, he had the strength to continue to pursue a full and active life, living alone in his small terraced house in Rectory Lane, but being very much part of the social and church activity of Somersham.

John was born in Oxford where his father held the post of Dean of Oriel College. He obtained a place to read classics at King's College, Cambridge, but war intervened and he joined the RAF in 1942. He flew as a navigator/bomb aimer in some 30 operations in Italy before his plane was shot down. He bailed out behind enemy lines, successfully hiding with an Italian family until he was eventually rescued, for his bravery he was mentioned in dispatches.

After the war he returned to King's to read theology, then went to a theological college and was ordained in 1948. He served as a priest in various churches. He later started writing crossword puzzles and The Guardian newspaper published the first of many in 1958. He eventually took to compiling crosswords full-time when his divorce in the late 1970s lost him his living as a clergyman (he was reinstated after the death of his first wife).

John's nom de plume, Araucaria, came from the botanical name for the monkey puzzle tree.

John Graham was made a Member of the Order of the British Empire in the 2005 New Year's Honours List for services to the newspaper industry. In July 2011 John was the guest on the BBC radio programme Desert Island Discs.

In December 2012 he revealed in a crossword puzzle that he had cancer of the oesophagus. He said that the puzzle had not taken him very long and that "It seemed the natural thing to do somehow," he said. "It just seemed right."

He did many anonymous acts of kindness, stealthily giving away much of his not very large income. He would write bespoke crosswords for people for several years before he died and passed the income to Somersham Church.

John died on 26th November 2013 and a service of thanksgiving and celebration for his life was held in January 2014 in Somersham Church. The Church was packed with members of John's family, people from the village as well as a number of famous people including Prince Michael of Kent and the actors Timothy West and Prunella Scales. The Bishop of Huntingdon gave the main address and other friends made oral tributes.

In 2018 Somersham's Parochial Church Council applied for permission to install a stone plaque in memory of John Graham. This was granted and the plaque was dedicated by the Bishop of Huntingdon at a special service in August that year. The plaque was paid for by donations and the excess was sufficient to pay for an oak cabinet to be bought and put towards the rear of the

Church Nave. New carpeting for the Lady Chapel and Memorial Corner was also purchased.

Revd Sue Simpson (Rector) and the Bishop of Huntingdon (David Thomson) after the service of dedication of the plaque.

HEREFORD HOUSE PAINTINGS

Over the years some interesting finds have been made in the Parish and I wrote about some of them in my book 'Somersham Heritage'. However, another one that relatively few people have seen are some wall paintings in the annexe (originally a granary and hayloft) of Hereford House in the High Street, the house owned by David and Ingrid Chambers. The paintings were discovered when rooms on the first floor were being re-decorated. They are painted directly on to the plaster and are believed to have been painted by one of the Wilson Daughters in 1887 as part of the celebrations for Queen Victoria's Golden Jubilee.

We know of those celebrations from an account of the proceedings which is taken from a local paper of June 25th, 1887. It begins: *"The Jubilee of her Majesty Queen Victoria will probably never be effaced from the memory of the inhabitants of Somersham, for it may safely be asserted that hardly ever, if at all, has there been unanimity of purpose to equal that exhibited on Tuesday. Long before the general public were astir a merry peal was rung on the Church bells, reminding all of the loyalty it was their duty and privilege to show during the day."*

Several generations of the Wilson family lived in Hereford House. Originally it is thought that the Rev. John Oakes Wilson claimed Hereford Farm during the Enclosure Act, when he was the Vicar in Somersham from 1764 – 1793. (Technically he was the Curate, the Rector of Somersham was in fact the Regius Professor of Divinity in Cambridge).

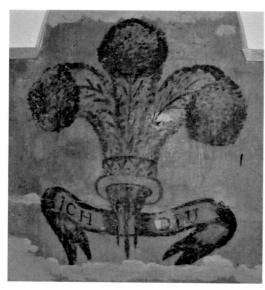

A few years ago, a descendant of the Wilson family came from Dorset to look at the 'family home'. They told Mr & Mrs Chambers that they have pictures painted by their Great Aunt dated in the 1880's and that she was quite a talented painter as can be seen from these pictures.

SOMERSHAM 1841

At the start of this book I wrote about the shops that used to be in Somersham. I am also fascinated by the people in the village and what they did. The earliest indication of this are the trades of people in the 1841 Census - the first one in which they are shown.

So here they are:

195 Agricultural Labourers
52 Female Servants
30 Pupils
29 Independent (means)
28 Farmers
15 Male Servants
11 Publicans
10 Bailiffs
10 Carpenters
9 Gardeners
7 Butchers
7 Shoemakers
7 Tailors
5 Blacksmiths
5 Dressmakers
5 Millers
5 Schoolmistresses
5 Shepherds
4 Match Men
4 Tramps
3 Apprentices
3 Bakers
3 Bricklayers
3 Cabinet Makers
3 Draper's Assistants
3 Drovers
2 Baker's Journeyman
2 Wheelwrights
2 Woodmen

3 Grocers
3 Innkeepers
3 Nurses
3 Surgeons
3 Tailor's Apprentices
3 Thatchers
2 Army Pensioners
2 Blacksmith Journeymen
2 Bonnet Maker Apprentices
2 Brewers
2 Carpenter Journeymen
2 Charwomen
2 Cooper Journeymen
2 Dressmaker's Apprentices
2 Glaziers
2 Horsebreakers
2 Ostlers
2 Rush Cutters
2 Rush Manufacturers
2 Sawyers
2 Schoolmasters
2 Shoemaker's Apprentices
2 Tailor Journeymen
2 Washerwomen
2 Watchmaker's Apprentices
1 In Army
1 Baptist Minister
1 Basket Maker
1 Basket Maker Journeyman

1 Bonnet Maker
1 Bricklayer's Labourer
1 Builder
1 Carrier
1 Coal Merchant
1 Collar Maker
1 Cooper
1 Cordwainer
1 Draper
1 Drillman
1 General Trade
1 Glazier Apprentice
1 Glazier Journeyman
1 Hairdresser
1 Horse Dealer
1 Huckster
1 Jobber
1 Joiner

1 Joiner's Journeyman
1 Labourer
1 Lodging Housekeeper
1 Machine Maker
1 Machine Man
1 Merchant
1 Minister
1 Postmistress
1 Poulterer
1 Rat Catcher
1 Scavenger
1 Schoolmistress Helper
1 Son's Housekeeper
1 Tailoress
1 Teacher
1 Toll Collector
1 Veterinary Surgeon
1 Watchmaker

It is not surprising that most people worked on the land, but 52 women were servants. The fact that Somersham had 10 Bailiffs, is perhaps surprising, although they were probably farmer's agents responsible for estate administration with duties such as collecting rents. It is interesting that there was a bonnet maker and a collar maker, however, it was usual for all women to wear a bonnet of some sort and collars were bought separately to sew on garments. The really amusing occupations are those of Scavenger and Tramp.

The Population of Somersham at that time was 1,517 (766 males and 751 females) in 300 dwellings. The trades indicate that Somersham was very 'self-contained'.

The 1911 Census is the most recent one in which we can access people's occupations. It still shows a similar number of people working on the land, but the bonnet maker and collar maker were no longer present, neither were the rat catcher, the tramps or the scavenger! However, new occupations were appearing with the spread of the railway and the move towards the use of new forms of machinery on the land. 39 people had occupations related to the railway, from platelayers to railway porters and clerks. There were 9 people whose work related to engine work in agriculture, they included drivers of traction engines and threshing machines. 12 people were employed with bakery, 13 with butchery, and 9 with dressmaking, all of which seems to indicate the presence of more shops. However, there were still 25 domestic servants. Education for all children had led to there being 142 school pupils.

An elderly gentleman that I interviewed a few years ago when talking about Somersham in the 1920s and 30s said " Life in the village was particularly parochial, not countywide or national. People were born in the village, went to school in the village, worked in the village, married in the village, brought their children up in the village and never left the village."

One can only guess as to the range of occupations in the 2011 Somersham Census, the latest one to be conducted. My guess would be a sharp decline in the number working in agriculture, because of the greater use of machinery, some of it being quite sophisticated. The increase in life expectancy has also led to more retired people.

Somersham has changed considerably over time, especially in the twentieth century. I am sure Somersham's future will continue to be of fascination and that is what makes the study of history so interesting.